SLAM DUNK PRONOUNS

By Doris Fisher and D. L. Gibbs
Cover illustrated by Scott Angle
Interior illustrated by Jeff Chandler
Curriculum consultant: Candia Bowles, M.Ed., M.S.

Gareth Stevens
Publishing

Please visit our web site at **www.garethstevens.com**.
For a free color catalog describing Gareth Stevens Publishing's list of
high-quality books, call 1-800-542-2595 (USA) or 1-800-387-3178 (Canada).
Gareth Stevens Publishing's fax: 1-877-542-2596

Library of Congress Cataloging-in-Publication Data

Fisher, Doris.
    Grammar all-stars / Doris Fisher and D. L. Gibbs.
      p. cm.
    ISBN-10: 0-8368-8904-5   ISBN-13: 978-0-8368-8904-8 (lib. bdg.)
    ISBN-10: 0-8368-8911-8   ISBN-13: 978-0-8368-8911-6 (pbk.)
    1. English language—Grammar—Juvenile literature. 2. English
language—Parts of speech—Juvenile literature. 3. Sports—Juvenile
literature. I. Gibbs, D.L. II. Title.
PE1112.F538   2008
428.2—dc22   2007033840

This edition first published in 2008 by
Gareth Stevens Publishing
A Weekly Reader® Company
1 Reader's Digest Road
Pleasantville, NY 10570-7000 USA

Senior Managing Editor: Lisa M. Guidone
Senior Editor: Barbara Bakowski
Creative Director: Lisa Donovan
Senior Designer: Keith Plechaty

Printed in the United States of America

1 2 3 4 5 6 7 8 9 10 09 08 07

CONTENTS

Look for the **boldface** words on each page.
Then read the **HOOPS HINT** that follows.

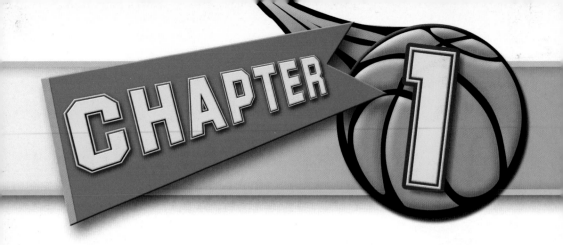

CHAPTER 1

READY FOR THE TIP-OFF

What Are Pronouns?

"Good afternoon, sports fans! **I** am Buzz Star for TV station P-L-A-Y, with today's championship game live from Rebound Arena. The Playmakers are taking on the Hotshots for this year's High Hoops Trophy. Kid reporter Jeff Turner has joined **me** in the broadcast booth. **He** will help call the play-by-play for this exciting championship game."

"Each team has already won a High Hoops championship," says Buzz. "Which team do **you** think will capture **its** second trophy, Jeff?"

"Just between **us**," says Jeff, "**I** think **it** will be the Hotshots. **They** have Bobby Bankshot on **their** team! **I** can't wait to see **him** play!"

"**I** wouldn't rule out the Playmakers," says Buzz. "**They** have Moochie Webb!"

"**His** sky hook is great," says Jeff, "but the Hotshots are **my** pick."

"Well, **we** have a big game on **our** hands today," says Buzz. "**I** hope **you** get to see **your** team win. Are **you** ready for the tip-off?"

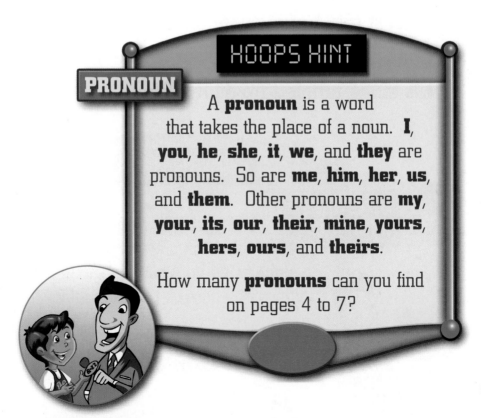

HOOPS HINT

PRONOUN

A **pronoun** is a word that takes the place of a noun. **I**, **you**, **he**, **she**, **it**, **we**, and **they** are pronouns. So are **me**, **him**, **her**, **us**, and **them**. Other pronouns are **my**, **your**, **its**, **our**, **their**, **mine**, **yours**, **hers**, **ours**, and **theirs**.

How many **pronouns** can you find on pages 4 to 7?

"**I** am ready!" says Jeff. "Basketball is **my** second-favorite sport."

"Second favorite?" asks Buzz. "Which sport do **you** like more?"

"**I** am the city yo-yo champion for ages twelve and under," says Jeff. "**I** perform all kinds of unusual tricks—Flying Saucer, Walk the Dog, and a lot of others. **You** should see **me** do Dizzy Baby! **I** practice at least two hours every day. **My** friend Chris practices with **me**, but **he** still gets **his** string tangled up all the time."

HOOPS HINT

SINGULAR PRONOUN

A **singular pronoun** takes the place of a singular noun. A singular noun names one person, place, or thing.

"All sports take a lot of practice, don't **they**?" asks Buzz.

"**They** do!" says Jeff. "But Mom and Dad think Chris and I spend too much time playing with **our** yo-yos and not enough time doing **our** homework. If **they** watched **us** practice, **they** would know **we** do both! **We** work hard to do better tricks—and to improve the grades on **our** tests. I help Chris learn yo-yo tricks, and he helps me learn all about pronouns."

"Oh, do you get your pronouns tangled up?" Buzz asks with a chuckle.

"I know what **they** are," says Jeff, "but I don't always use **them** correctly."

"Using pronouns is something like coaching basketball," says Buzz. "Coaches have to decide when to take out **their** starters and replace **them** with players from the bench. In a sentence, you have to decide when to take out nouns and replace **them** with pronouns."

"That sounds like a slam dunk!" says Jeff.

HOOPS HINT

PLURAL PRONOUN

A **plural pronoun** takes the place of a plural noun.

"Just remember," says Buzz, "that a
coach has to select the right substitute. The
second-string player has to do the same job
as the starter who's being replaced."

14

"So in a sentence, you have to use a pronoun that agrees with the noun it replaces," says Jeff.

Buzz nods. "There's the tip-off, folks!"

CHAPTER 2

THEY CALL IT A GAME
Subject and Object Pronouns

"**We** can take turns calling the action, Jeff," says Buzz. "**You** take the Hotshots. **I** will take the Playmakers."

"OK," says Jeff. "**I** hope **I** can keep up with the players. **They** move so fast!

"Air Duke has possession of the ball. **He** races downcourt and passes it to teammate Dan Dunkin. Dunkin drives toward the basket, and **he** shoots a layup. The ball is circling the rim, and **it** finally drops in. **He** scores!"

"**It** is your turn now, Mr. Star," says Jeff. "How did **I** do?"

"Well, **you** certainly used a lot of pronouns!" Buzz replies. "Just remember that the 'player' a pronoun replaces has to be clear. **You** don't want to confuse the fans."

"**I** don't want to confuse *myself*!"

HOOPS HINT

SUBJECT
PRONOUN

A **subject pronoun** replaces a noun that is a subject in a sentence. A subject noun tells **who** is doing something or **what** the sentence is about.

"Just listen to **me** for a while," says Buzz, "and don't worry. You'll get **it**.

"Billy Backcourt has the ball for the Playmakers. Backcourt is dribbling, but he's almost standing still. The Hotshots' defense is surrounding **him**. Moochie Webb is open, and he is heading toward the basket. Webb is waving his arms and signaling for the ball. Backcourt finally notices **him**. Two defenders are in Backcourt's face, but he bounces the ball between **them**. Ken Weaver grabs the ball and passes **it** to Webb, who shoots and misses. He rebounds and shoots again. 'Look sharp, Webb!' shouts the Playmakers' coach. 'Get **us** some points. The fans are depending on **you**.' Webb's third shot is a slam dunk!"

"I've got **it**," says Jeff, taking over.

"Bankshot hustles the ball to the sideline and passes **it** to Duke. Duke drills through the defense, but Weaver stays on **him**. Duke shoots, and Weaver fouls **him**. Now they line up for the free throw. Duke gets two shots. The first shot is … GOOD! He shoots again and … SWISH!"

HOOPS HINT

OBJECT PRONOUN

An **object pronoun** receives the action in a sentence. It usually follows the verb. It can also come after words such as **about**, **around**, **between**, **at**, **for**, **in**, **of**, **on**, **to**, and **with**.

21

"I told you the Hotshots are going to win," Jeff says to Buzz. "They have the lead. The Playmakers will never catch them before the buzzer. It's almost halftime."

Buzz grins. "You did pretty well for a rookie," he says. "There's the buzzer, folks. The score at halftime is Hotshots 42, Playmakers 38."

CHAPTER 3

WHOSE SHOT IS IT?

Possessive Pronouns

"For those fans who are just tuning in," says Buzz, "**our** game is in **its** fourth quarter. The Playmakers were trailing at the half, but they bounced back in the third period. **Their** lead has been going up and down like a yo-yo!

"And speaking of yo-yos, **my** kid reporter, Jeff Turner, just lost **his** yo-yo. When Air Duke made the tie-breaking three-point shot, Jeff jumped out of **his** seat. **His** yo-yo fell out of his pocket

and tumbled into the stands. I see Jeff
returning to the booth now.

"Did you find **your** yo-yo?" asks Buzz.

"A woman found it for me," says
Jeff. "It was under **her** seat. Did I miss
anything?"

"No. The Playmakers just used **their** last time-out," says Buzz. "The Hotshots have the ball, so it's **your** turn to announce the play-by-play."

"OK," says Jeff. "Halfcourt inbounds the ball to Bankshot, who passes to Duke."

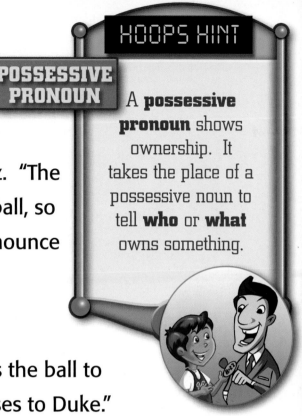

"Duke is streaking downcourt. Oh, no! The referee calls Duke for traveling, so the Playmakers get the ball back.

"Moochie Webb drives toward the lane, but Duke blocks him. With two seconds on the clock, Webb shoots from midcourt. The ball rebounds off the backboard. I hear the buzzer—my team wins!"

"With a final score of 85 to 82, the Hotshots have earned their second High Hoops Trophy," says Buzz. "Jeff, you did a great job."

"Thanks," says Jeff. "I enjoyed being your kid reporter. Will you come to my next yo-yo contest?"

Buzz grins. "If you ask me, I will even be its announcer," he says.

HOOPS HINT

PRONOUNS

How well do you know the rules? See how many **pronouns** you can find on pages 28 to 29.

BUZZ STAR PLAYS BY THE RULES!

 A **pronoun** takes the place of a noun.
Examples: Buzz likes basketball games. **He** announces **them**.

 A **singular pronoun** takes the place of a singular noun, which names only one person or one thing.
Examples: Jeff practices yo-yo tricks daily. **He** wants to win contests.

 A **plural pronoun** takes the place of a plural noun, which names more than one person or one thing.
Example: Jeff and Buzz announce the basketball game. **They** take turns calling the action.

 A **subject pronoun** is a subject in a sentence. The seven subject pronouns are **I**, **we**, **you**, **he**, **she**, **it**, and **they**.
Examples: Chris is Jeff's best friend. **He** helps Jeff learn pronouns. Bobby Bankshot and Ken Weaver are basketball centers. **They** are very tall.

 An **object pronoun** receives the action in a sentence. The seven object pronouns are **me**, **us**, **you**, **him**, **her**, **it**, and **them**.
Examples: When Moochie Webb has the ball, he shoots **it**. A woman found Jeff's yo-yo. She gave **it** to **him**.

 A **possessive pronoun** shows ownership.
The **possessive pronouns** are **my**, **mine**, **your**, **yours**, **his**, **her**, **hers**, **its**, **our**, **ours**, **their**, and **theirs**.
Examples: **My** turn is first. Please wait for **yours**.
Dan Dunkin pulled hard on the basket. Now **its** net is torn.

ALL-STAR ACTIVITY

Jeff read his class a report about the basketball game.
Can you find all the singular and plural pronouns?

I was with Buzz Star at Rebound Arena on Saturday. He is a TV announcer, and I helped him. We took turns. The Hotshots played the Playmakers in the biggest basketball game of the season. Its prize was the huge High Hoops Trophy. Both teams really wanted to win it!

The players ran up and down the court very fast. I had to keep up with them. They dribbled and passed and shot the ball fast, too. Seeing Air Duke make a three-point shot was the best part of the game. When I stood up to cheer, my yo-yo fell and rolled into the stands. A woman found it under her seat. When she gave the yo-yo back to me, I did my Flying Saucer trick for her. Then she tried it, too. The people near us must have liked our show. They clapped for us.

The Playmakers won the trophy—their second win! After the game, Bobby Bankshot gave me his autograph. Some other players sent theirs along to all of you.

On a piece of paper, list all the **singular pronouns** in Jeff's report. Then list all the **plural pronouns**.

All-Star
Challenge

Label each pronoun on your list as **subject**, **object**, or **possessive**.

Turn the page to check your answers and to see how many extra points you scored.

ANSWER KEY

Did you find enough pronouns to score a slam dunk?

0–7 pronouns: Traveling (oops!)   **16–23** pronouns: Free Throw

8–15 pronouns: Rebound   **24–30** pronouns: SLAM DUNK!

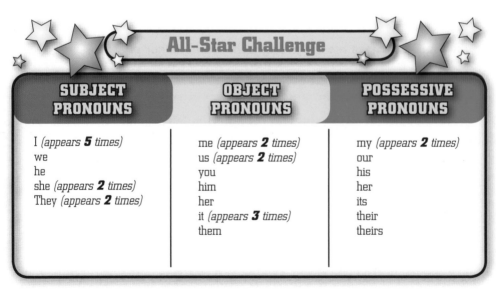

SINGULAR PRONOUNS			PLURAL PRONOUNS	
1. I	**9.** my	**17.** she	**21.** we	**29.** theirs
2. he	**10.** it	**18.** it	**22.** them	**30.** you
3. I	**11.** her	**19.** me	**23.** they	
4. him	**12.** she	**20.** his	**24.** us	
5. Its	**13.** me		**25.** our	
6. it	**14.** I		**26.** they	
7. I	**15.** my		**27.** us	
8. I	**16.** her		**28.** their	

All-Star Challenge

SUBJECT PRONOUNS	OBJECT PRONOUNS	POSSESSIVE PRONOUNS
I (appears **5** times)	me (appears **2** times)	my (appears **2** times)
we	us (appears **2** times)	our
he	you	his
she (appears **2** times)	him	her
They (appears **2** times)	her	its
	it (appears **3** times)	their
	them	theirs